Brilliant Bees

Brilliant Bees

By Linda Glaser
Illustrated by Gay W. Holland

The Millbrook Press   Brookfield, Connecticut

To my dear friend Kevin, a brilliant gardener,
passionate nature lover, and buddy extraordinaire.
L.G.

To Connie, for always being there
with love and encouragement.
G.W.H.

Library of Congress Cataloging-in-Publication Data
Glaser, Linda.
Brilliant bees / by Linda Glaser ; illustrated by Gay W. Holland.
p. cm.
Summary: Simple text and illustrations describe the physical
characteristics, habits, and life cycle of the honey bee.
ISBN 0-7613-2670-7 (lib. bdg.)
ISBN 0-7613-1943-3 (pbk.)
1. Honeybee—Juvenile literature. [1. Honeybee. 2. Bees.]
I. Holland, Gay W., ill. II. Title.
QL568.A6 G53 2003 595.79'9—dc21 2001008630

Published by The Millbrook Press, Inc.
2 Old New Milford Road
Brookfield, Connecticut 06804
www.millbrookpress.com

Printed in the United States of America
5 4 3 2 1 (lib.)
5 4 3 2 1 (pbk.)

A honeybee lands lightly on a flower.
She sips the sweet nectar with her long, thin tongue.
Look! She spots a whole cluster of nectar-filled blossoms.

She flies straight home to let her hive know.
But how will one little honeybee
show all the others just where to go?

She dances a brilliant bee dance.
She loops around in a figure eight
and waggles her body.
Shake, shake, shake.

The bees touch and smell her
with their sensitive feelers.
Her dance tells them
where the flowers are,
which way to go,
and exactly how far.

The flowers are more than a mile away,
but the honeybees easily find the way.

Their see-through wings hum
as they busily fly from blossom to blossom.

Sip, sip, sip. They collect sweet nectar.
And as they do, they carry yellow pollen
on furry legs and bodies
from one flower to another.

Carrying pollen from flower to flower
helps the plants form fruits and seeds.
This is called pollination.
It's one big job of honeybees.

Now the bees brush pollen into tiny baskets
on their back legs. And they collect nectar
in a special stomach called a honey sac.

When they're full, they fly straight home
to store it all in their honeycomb.

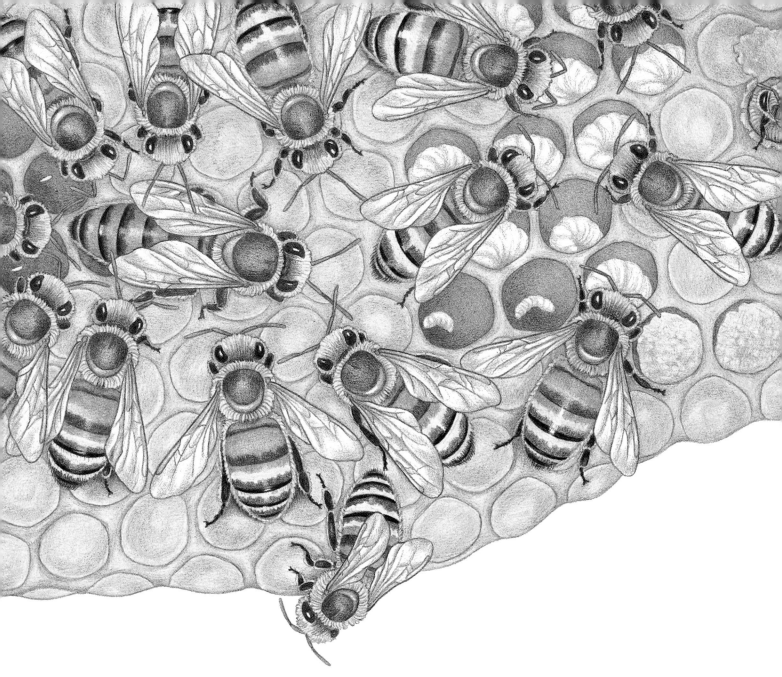

Inside the hive, thousands of honeybees work smoothly
together—helping each other stay alive.
Some bees clean and polish the hive.
Others build wax cells—each with six perfect sides.

The cells are built with an upward tilt
so the sweet nectar doesn't drip or spill.
Some bees fan the nectar. How?
With their wings!
Slowly, it thickens and turns into rich, yummy honey.

Others guard and
protect the hive.
They sting if an animal
comes too close.
So I'm careful to stay
a safe distance away.

Some bees feed the babies,
and others feed the one queen bee.

The queen's only job is to lay
thousands of eggs day after day.

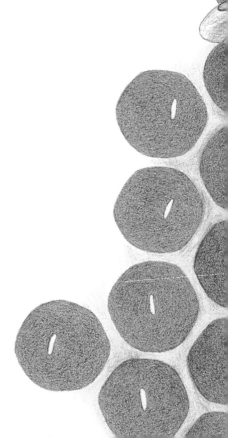

The eggs grow quickly.
Soon they change completely—
from soft larva babies
into full-grown honeybees.

The new bees join right in with the hive—
working smoothly together
to keep the colony alive.

Honeybees are brilliant dancers,
builders, and honey makers,
and most important, pollinators.

Many, many plants and trees
are pollinated by honeybees:

Apples, apricots, avocados, cherries,
strawberries, raspberries, grapes, and blueberries,
peaches, pears, watermelons, plums,
cranberries, cantaloupes, cucumbers, and almonds.

We have lots of reasons to thank the bees—
for honey and beeswax
and for helping plants form
fruits and seeds.

Thank you, little honeybees.

H

ere are the answers to some questions you may have about honeybees.

QUEEN

DRONE

WORKER

How many honeybees live in a hive?
There can be over 50,000 honeybees in one hive. All of them have jobs that help keep the hive running smoothly. There is one queen bee. She is the biggest bee in the hive. Her job is to lay eggs. The male bees are called drones. Their only job is to mate with the queen bee. This helps make new baby bees for the hive. Most bees in the hive are female worker bees. Workers do many different jobs—from cleaning the hive to feeding babies to gathering nectar, pollen, and water for the hive. As they grow older, worker bees move from one job to another.

What job does a worker bee do first?
A worker's first job is to clean and polish the hive. When she gets a little older, she feeds and cares for the baby larvae. Next, she helps build new six-sided wax cells for the honeycomb. Workers also help feed and care for the queen, store pollen and nectar, and fan the nectar with their wings so it thickens into honey. In hot weather, workers help cool the hive by fanning their wings. Older workers guard the entrance to the hive. The worker's last job is to go outside and collect nectar, pollen, and water for her hive.

How do honeybees use nectar and pollen?
Nectar and pollen and the foods made from them, such as honey, are the only foods that honeybees eat.

How long do honeybees live?
In the summer, worker bees may live about 20 to 40 days. In the winter, they may live four to six months. Drones live from four to eight weeks. The queen may live from three to five years.

How do bees carry pollen from flower to flower?
When a honeybee collects nectar from a flower, pollen gets caught on the branched hairs of her legs and body. When she goes to the next flower, some of the pollen brushes onto that flower. In this way, bees move pollen from flower to flower. This is called pollination. When pollen lands on a flower, it helps the flower to form new seeds. Without honeybees, many plants and trees would not be able to form new seeds.

Why do bees dance?
Honeybees dance to communicate with each other about the location of flowers. They do a circle dance to show that flowers are close by. They do a waggle dance in a figure eight to show that flowers are over 300 feet away. They have other dances as well. Some of these dances aren't understood by people yet.

How many flowers does a honeybee visit in a day?
During the summer a honeybee may visit 10,000 flowers in one day!

How much honey does one honeybee make?
In her whole life, one honeybee collects enough nectar to make about a teaspoon of honey.

Do honeybees visit many different types of flowers in one day?
Usually not. Honeybees prefer to collect nectar from only one type of flower at a time. For example, if flowers are plentiful, honeybees may visit only cherry trees for a few weeks. During that time all those cherry trees are pollinated.

Where do honeybees get wax to build the honeycomb?
The wax is formed inside them. It comes out of openings in their abdomen.

How do people use beeswax?
It's used to make beeswax candles and some cosmetics.

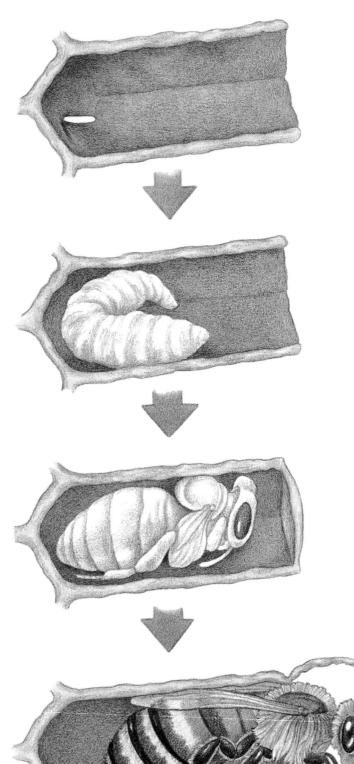

What do baby bees look like?
Baby bees hatch from small white eggs. First, a bee is a small, white, wormlike larva.

The larva grows much bigger and changes into a white pupa. Finally, the pupa forms a cocoon and changes into a full-grown honeybee. We call these changes "metamorphosis." A worker bee grows from egg to adult bee in about twenty-one days.

Why do bees sting?
Bees need to be able to protect themselves. They sting only if they think they are in danger or if the hive is in danger. So, when you watch bees, always stay a safe distance away from them and their hive.

If a honeybee stings, does it die?
Yes. Worker bees have stingers with barbs. The stinger stays in the victim. Since the stinger is part of the bee's body, when the bee loses its stinger, it dies.

Are bee stings dangerous?
For most people, bee stings aren't dangerous. However, some people are allergic to bee stings. For them, it could be very serious. If a bee ever stings you, tell a grown-up.

Are there other bees besides honeybees?
Yes. There are about 20,000 types of bees in the world besides honeybees.

Where in the world do bees live?
They live everywhere on Earth except for the Arctic and Antarctica.

Where do bees go in winter?
In cold climates, during the winter, female honeybees stay inside the hive. The drones (males) are pushed out before winter, since there wouldn't be enough food for them. The rest of the honeybees huddle together, all taking turns in the center in order to stay warm.

What makes a bee buzz?
The wings of a bee move very fast—11,400 times per minute. That is what makes the buzzing sound.

Where do honeybees make their hives?
Bees live in dark places. In the wild, they often make hives in hollow trees. Since the 1850s, beekeepers have cared for bees in box-shaped hives with movable frames, invented by Reverend Lorenzo Langstrothowadays. Many honeybees live in these hives. But there are still wild bees as well.

For more information on honeybees, visit these Web sites:
http://www.pbs.org/wgbh/nova/bees
http://www.honey.com/kids/facts

Why are honeybees important?
Honeybees supply people around the world with honey. Every year, bees supply people with about 1,000,000 tons of honey. But even more important for the Earth, honeybees pollinate trees, wildflowers, fields, and gardens. Many plants, trees, crops, and flowers that give us food and make the world beautiful depend on little honeybees to survive.

How can people help honeybees?
Garden organically, without using pesticides or herbicides on the lawn or garden.

Buy organic foods—grown without pesticides and herbicides. Pesticides and herbicides are poisons that kill many harmless and often helpful creatures, including honeybees. Organic gardening and shopping help honeybees stay alive and healthy so that they can do their important work of pollinating flowers, plants, and trees around the world.

About the Author and Artist

Linda Glaser is the author of many successful nonfiction picture books on natural history subjects. Her books *Wonderful Worms, Compost!, Spectacular Spiders,* and *Our Big Home: An Earth Poem* were all named Outstanding Science Trade Books for Children by The Children's Book Council/National Science Teachers Association. *Our Big Home: An Earth Poem* is also featured on Reading Rainbow, the national PBS television show. In addition to writing, Ms. Glaser conducts writing workshops for schoolchildren, teachers, and other adults. She lives in Minnesota.

Illustrator Gay W. Holland has been fascinated with nature ever since she was a child. She has illustrated two other Linda Glaser books, *Magnificent Monarchs* and *Spectacular Spiders.* She is the author and illustrator of another recent Millbrook title, *Look Closer: An Introduction to Bug-Watching.*